1/20

PUPPY MIND

PUPPY MIND

Andrew Jordan Nance

ILLUSTRATED BY

Jim Durk

PLUM BLOSSOM
BOOKS

BERKELEY, CALIFORNIA

Thank you to everyone at Parallax Press; my wonderful family; Jim Durk, a true artist; J.G. Larochette, founder of Mindful Life Project; Stacey Gonzalez, teacher extraordinaire; and the entire staff and student body of San Francisco's Charles Drew Academy. I am so grateful to all of you for your guidance and partnership.

PLUM BLOSSOM BOOKS

Plum Blossom Books, the children's imprint of Parallax Press, publishes books on mindfulness for young people and the grown-ups in their lives.

Parallax Press
P.O. Box 7355
Berkeley, California 94707
parallax.org

For help in training your Puppy Mind go to: **www.mindfulartssf.org**

Library of Congress Cataloging-in-Publication Data is available upon request.

3 4 5 / 19 18 17

To your Puppy Mind.
Please be kind.

My mind is like a puppy,
it likes to wander and explore.

If I don't watch it carefully
it goes through any open door.

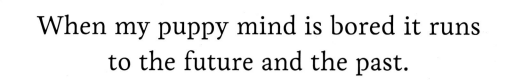

When my puppy mind is bored it runs
to the future and the past.

If I am not really careful,
it will take me far away super fast.

My puppy mind can dig up memories,
like when I got yelled at for not sharing my things.

My mind scampers to the future
and I don't always like the
pictures that it brings.

In class I try to listen to the teacher,
but my puppy mind starts to stir.
I quickly lose my focus,
and the day becomes a blur.

I get mad at my puppy mind,
"Why don't you just sit and stay!"

When I yell my puppy mind
gets scared and hides or runs away.

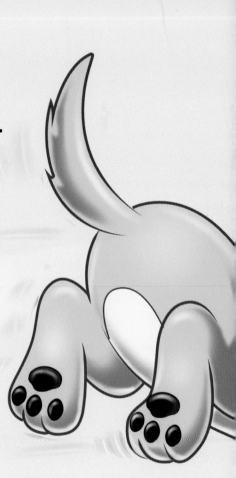

My puppy mind only heels
if I take three slow deep breaths.
If I do it often enough, I feel calmer in my chest.

Taking three slow breaths
is the best way to train my puppy mind.
I am learning to be my mind's best friend.
It responds best when I am kind.

So whenever I feel my puppy mind
tugging at my sleeve,
I try to remember . . .

to breathe and breathe and breathe.

If I practice breathing every day,
and remember to be kind,
I will have more fun being with
my best friend, my playful puppy mind.